Seasons
Lost and Found

Seasons Lost and Found

Shelley Kahn

Seasons Lost and Found
Copyright © 2021 Shelley Kahn
ISBN: 978-0-578-88334-2
Library of Congress Control Number: 2021911130

All rights reserved under the International and Pan-American Copyright Conventions. No part of this book by be reproduced in any manner whatsoever without written permission from the Publisher, except in the case of brief quotations embodied in critical articles and reviews.

Shelley Kahn is employed in federal service as a civil rights attorney. She lives in the suburbs of Washington, D.C., but her heart pulls her to the Delaware coast. Her poems have been featured in Melancholy Hyperbole, Dove Tales, The Path and other publications. She is a member of the Rehoboth Beach Writer's Guild.

Cover illustration/design & interior illustrations by: Emily Hunter

Interior layout/design by: Crystal Heidel, Byzantium Sky Press

The following poems have previously appeared in the publications noted below:

"Late Birthday" appeared in From the Depths, "Journeys", Winter 2013-14, *Haunted Waters Press*

"My Parade" appeared in *Melancholy Hyperpole*, November 2013

"Rusty Dreams" appeared in *Melancholy Hyperbole*, November 2013

"Holiday Cheer" appeared in *Moon Magazine*, January 2014

"Mother and Daughter" appeared in *The White Space*, Chapbook by Rehoboth Beach Writers Guild, April 2015

"Night Terrors" appeared *The White Space*, Chapbook by Rehoboth Beach Writers Guild, April 2015

"Excising Guilt from Morning Rituals" appeared in 2014 *Write to Woof Anthology* by Grey Wolfe Publications, LLC.

"Frenchie Love" appeared in 2014 *Write to Woof Anthology* by Grey Wolfe Publications, LLC.

"Cyclone" appeared in *The Path Literary Magazine*, published as "A Bad Night to Remember", Winter 2013

"Migration" appeared on my writer's page for the Rehoboth Beach Writers Guild, February 2013

"In the Garden" appeared on my writer's page for the Rehoboth Beach Writers Guild, also in "Joyful," October 2010.

"Day and Night" appeared on my writer's page for the Rehoboth Beach Writers Guild, February 2013

"Photography" appeared in *Dove Tales anthology*, 2014 by Writing for Peace

"Pack Rat" appeared in *The Broadkill Review*, April/May 2015

Table of Contents

Autumn 1
   Breath 3
   Unveiling (At the crematorium) 4
   Late Birthday 5
   Ode to October 7
   Fall from Grace 8
   October Morning at Green Spring Gardens 9
   Butternut squash soup 10
   never tastes right 10
   My Parade 11
   Flower Children 13
   "You can't take it with you…" 15
   Storm Walk 16
   Morning Near the Beach 18

Winter 19
   Holiday Cheer 21
   After the Storm 22
   How to Survive in Winter 23
   My Daughter 24
   Rusty Dreams 25
   Morning Rituals 27
   Frenchie Love 28
   Teaching the Dog to Pee on the Deck 29
   Winter Walk 31

Spring 33
   Anthem 35
   Migration 37
   In Love 38

Opera of the Soul 39
My Muse 40
In the Garden 41
Rosebud 42
Beginning 43
Batter Up! 44
Photography 45
Pandemic Praise Song 46

Summer 49
  Workaday Plea 51
  Something is Coming 52
  Spider Land 55
  Off the Boardwalk 56
  French Fry Finality 58
  Celestial Ground Search 59
  Envy 62
  Holes 63
  Day and Night 65
  Foreboding 66
  Cyclone 67
  Night Terrors 69
  Pack Rat 70
  To Walt Whitman 72
  Resolution 73

Acknowledgements

This initial poetry chapbook is the product of many years of writing (since childhood) and is hopefully the first of others to come. I owe so much gratitude to the many kind individuals who helped me along the way to its conclusion-from my relatives and friends who indulged me by reading my work (including my patient husband Gene), Emily Hunter, who drew such lovely graphic art, and so many of my fellow poets in the wonderful Rehoboth Beach Writer's Guild, who taught me (Ethan Joella and Gail Comorat), edited my work (Ellen Collins), and helped me with its final publication (Crystal Heidel).

My hope for this first effort is only that it is read by those for whom it will resonate. For it is my abiding view that resonance, even in our darkest moments, is what life's journey is all about.

Breath

In the silence of the night
our mother took her last breath
moving out of this world into the next.

That final time I saw her
the neat hospital bedding was so white
around her pale yellowed face.

I will not forget that feeling in my hotel room,
suddenly waking.
My sister said it was so quiet.

I picture the exhale of air
escaping into the cosmic otherness.
A black hole still sucking the grief out of my gut.

Unveiling (At the crematorium)

Blow away the world
It is far too hard to hold

Close your eyes and feel
How death was meant to heal

Forget the wind that spills
Ashes through window sills

Filling the darkest space
With memories so unreal

Open wide the still yawning urn
Vacant with hope's last appeal

Find meaning in all that is left
Want everything, still bereft.

Late Birthday

On the 23rd of October-
The stale birthday cake is an ode
To the memories and empty air.
My sister remembers those days
In her inner heart, as the dark
Pervades her home, she dreams
Of those old days
We celebrated all together.

I tighten my grasp of cards
We still write every year.
After each tear
She cries again.
Sometime later, we motor to the Florida condo
Sucking the air from the highway
Sewing our flowers shut.
We taste Mom's cake again this year
A labor of love, if always
Garish, harbinger of hard times.
Ahead, the gardens
Teeming like champagne.
We drive by a hobo sitting there
At the roadside smoking.
She gave everything to us
We don't drop our gaze
Or pause to fill his cup.
These sad times seem forever.
Our mother sleeps in the dust.
But on the road, I see her now.
Blink. And she is gone. That last birthday

Heading into a long sleep
Through barrows of loam and cold.
It is a clear enough story.
We want to bake her cake,
Saying blow those candles out
And let's get back to loving her once again
But we never can.

Ode to October

The leaves will still fall

The moon will grow large
Hanging limpid above

Everything alive ends with a frost.

As if it were really written—
In that great big Jewish book

We suddenly see our
Pursuit of the next season

Cut painfully short and rendered grim
By a late diagnosis, an earnest look

So many things die off in the Fall.

Fall from Grace

As rain ferments the leaves outside my window, I recall
    the sound they make when they fall so far from grace.

Turned loose from the sheltering bough they leaned upon
    during the light filled warmer months of Summer,

when, green with anticipation and longing they waved with joy,
    today they are still and chaste in marble veined colors.

Just like an encapsulated whisper of distress
    I feel the slightest exhale of nature dying.

I never noticed much before.

But I can feel it when the rainy, leaf blown season starts,
    and it is raining everywhere beyond my door.

October Morning at Green Spring Gardens

No dogs allowed
In the garden beds,
The small sign proclaims.

The ground parches
In the harsh sunlight
Where browning leaves
Are left to curl where they fall

But the tired marigolds
Wave their still green stems
At the small dog,
Releasing their
Almost spent scent.

She nuzzles them
With a wet nose
And they know,
Their season
Has not yet ended.

*Butternut squash soup
never tastes right*

Except in the Fall
When it is sublime.
We almost taste the colors
Of the turning leaves
In the bowl,
A golden oak hue as a base,
With a swirl of reddish maple
Folded into its essence,
Disappearing on your spoon.

My Parade

I remember
That Thanksgiving day winter white dress
So short with its fur edging and ties
With fur balls at the ends.
I twirled them in tandem,
waiting to watch the parade pass by.
From our apartment window.

I remember
My father's conflicted face
As he laughed at my finery
While my mother lay still and silent in a darkened room
Waiting for the pain to pass along
With the procession moving ever closer
So incongruous,
From our apartment window.

I remember my impatience
My long gone mother's hand
On my hair as she tugged the brush
Through and placed a single barrette there.
I blew short breaths over my hands
To dry my nail polish as I waited for
The slowly moving Underdog balloon
To gently fill the air outside
Our apartment window.

I remember now
They asked me why
I stood by the window
When I could
View the spectacle quite well
On our living room tv.
After all,
Didn't I know
We lived in Queens, not Manhattan,
So there was no chance I would see
The parade from there.

I remember well that first taste
Of disappointment
That aching regret that
Imperfections existed everywhere.
Even while we gave thanks and ate a special meal
Even in my winter white fur trimmed dress
My mother lay ill and Underdog was absent
From the atmosphere.

Outside our apartment window
After dinner in the cooling autumn air
Even though I harbored hope for a miracle,
Only emptiness was waiting for me there.

Flower Children

Greta sat in the sun sometimes.
They talked a bit of gardens and empty nests
Of grandchildren, Ivy League Schools and recent tests.
Her neighbor, Grace, edged each day
Unto her weathered bench next door, eyeing
Her hydrangeas every morning,
Wondering to herself if they were so colorful
Because she had a green thumb,
Or if she spoke to them at times like children
When Grace was not around to see them.
Her plants turned toward the light so nearly prone
Welcoming her attentions as if she were their mother
Opening their buds to her as if-
There were nothing left on earth to fear.

Though Grace gave all she had,
Watering and singing to their roots,
Her own plants never approached her neighbor's
Vivid hues and warmed leaves.
Even when the weather turned to New England chill
In late September, even as the blood moon eclipsed,
She envied that profusion of magenta and greenish
    alabaster
So ripe with color, just short of rotting on the vine.
As she said her good morning
And thanked the universe
She had woken up once again.

Even while she waited for her own children to drive her,
In their ramshackle cars past their untended homes nearby,
For appointments, not for coffee or lunch,
She envied the signs of growth next door,
The flowers bobbing their heads in all directions tied in a bunch.
But only Grace was there one fine early morning,
When her neighbor's bench sat empty under the eaves,
Waiting in the moon chilled air for her friend to emerge,
Seemingly as she gazed,
The flowers turned a slight brown.
The wilt on them grew more pronounced
In a way Greta would never have permitted
Even if she needed to fuel them with her own blood.

Across town, visitors approached her neighbor's last bed.
Greta looked at peace they whispered,
The flowers bled colors beside her
Waving at her form still expectant of her love
Greta will be here soon, they said
But they are this day disappointed
Their stems now cut, they will not last long
And Grace waits with rare patience on her bench
For the flower children beside her empty home to fade away.

"You can't take it with you..."

(From title of 1938 movie, playwrights Moss Hart
and George S. Kaufman, directed by Frank Capra)

I packed a life yesterday, and then,
When it was complete
And everything was boxed up securely
With almost an entire roll of that special tape
So sticky and difficult to unravel,
I could not remember where I placed
The most precious item of all:
A beautiful bowl that had for so long resided
In my elegant mother-in-law's china cabinet.
Like a heart, it was made of multifaceted crystal parts
With soft red rose petals within.

At night I dreamed
That it beat a steady rhythm
locked in one of the cardboard boxes
I so carefully packed.

Today, I remember the last time I saw her
The warmth in her eyes, that extra long hug,
How she trusted us to bring her home from that place intact.

She had such impeccable taste.
But no amount of packing tape
Can bring her heart back.

Storm Walk

Morning light shows leaves on the deck
in a random yellow pattern,
pressed flat and dampening
the grey wood planks on which they rest.

Random twisted branches litter our porch and
the hint of a fecund odor wafts through the air.

Inside, vacant air waits for the slightest thing to move.
The only sound is that appliance related hum
of our washer chugging phosphates.

So we take our dog to the beach to watch the swells
erode the newly shorn beach cliffs.
High tides nip at the edge of protective dunes.
Moulted ghost crab shells line our pathways.

I am a detective on our walks,
noticing the salt burn on the evergreens,
the cotton blossoms wafting in the air,
wondering where all the rabbits have gone.

Tired at last, I pause at our tiny dock,
eventually admitting to myself,
I see the scrim of something
floating on the water.

When we return, all is quiet,
though the dryer still beats
its cyclical hum.
Nothing to be done,
these last free days.

Morning Near the Beach

Waking, I hear and imagine the rain,
Seeping into the cracks of my dry bones
As I shakily rise from my bed.
Opening the blinds I see
Everything outside our door
Awaits dismemberment in the coming storm.

Green leafy canopies still hold sway in October's chill.
A veritable garden of earthy delight, spent blooms
    abounding,
Punctuates our walk in the streaming open faucet
Wall of water. After coffee, eschewing rain boots,
We take a turn on the blacktop path,
Noticing small frogs dancing in the muddy puddles
And birds drinking it all in from the trees above—
Still safe in their nests. While they prepare for
The take off and the long journey,
Acorns bombard the roof and
Squirrels dare the dog to give chase and
I wonder—how many beats of wing it will take
For the birds to reach their southern destinations.
I dream of traveling with them
Long before the pelting rain
Turns to frost and ice.

Holiday Cheer

Do not tell me to shine my light into a dark room.
I prefer the absence of such interventions
To pedantic purpose and tithed out virtue.

Do not ask me to confess anything to you either.
I long ago opened the hollowed out cage of my heart
Emptied its still beating contents in a sieve
And went on my way to the soup kitchen
To eat hearty with my true friends,
While Yuletide chilled the empty altar to excess
With its gaily wrapped boxes chock filled
With nothing we really need or want.

Especially don't ask me to make fruitless visits
To long ago causes that still make my face burn
As if I really believed in them…

It is too late to cook for the masses anyway,
The cookies are burned, the gift wrap torn,
The little boy at my door with his list
Turned away empty handed.
The coins I would give him
Shrivel in my pocket as I
Toss away my cellphone
And ring the women's shelter by land line instead.
Talking truth to a desperate human being, I find
Merry times speed past when we redeem each other
And leave both hypocrisy and sainthood behind.

After the Storm

Snow in my nose is cold and stifling.
Snow on my hands is like white ice cream,
it sticks and freezes in place.

Snow underfoot is sometimes like wading
through Captain Crunch cereal drifts,
sharp and crackling beneath my boots,
pounding down its texture.

Snow in my mouth can even feel tasteless and dry,
freezing my heart with
tentacles of cold ash.

Snow every day is like mind hibernation.
Thinking draws down slowly to whiteness,
blinding the eyes—
stopping the ears
with wet plugs of ice.

Even dreams cease to be.
They are pillow soft,
a soundless white landscape,
in the never ending snow world
inside of me.

How to Survive in Winter

Show love to those you care for.
Eat oranges to ward against cold.
Give thanks for warm blankets and
The cool wet nose of your dog friend.
Feel the wind and hear the birds.
Listen to the working gears of
Public servants grinding
Cares into dust.
Bless the New Year,
Curse the old ways
Make a thousand resolutions,
You will not keep.
See your mother and father hold hands
Before the snowfall
That takes them away.
Feel the last sound of their voices
Reverberate in your bones, and
Forge ahead.
Know they will meet you there.

My Daughter

(After Pablo Neruda and Nancy Pagh)

I like to love you still,
Even after you returned
My warm kisses
With icicle laden air
You keep around for show.
I like that in dreams

You come to me with hugs
On a dark winter morning
When birds no longer fly.
Yet all things still
Seem possible.

You sleep like the unborn babies
I never birthed. No other child for me
Ever lived but you, although my son still comes
Quickly when I call, I cannot give him
What you would not take.

I like to wake - with the words still on my lips,
Mom or Mommy, never Mother.
I still freeze in that icebox you made me
No chance to defrost my limbs.
I like to hope for you still

To greet me with endearments
You have reserved for another.
Maybe in the way a pollinated flower
Leaves seeds behind,
We will find each other again.

Rusty Dreams

Her earlier visions of happiness were
Far from the reality
Of that purgatory place she inhabits.
Less than what she dreamed it would be
In the infancy of her longed for independence.
Her personal trailer park of abandoned aspirations
Rusts alongside the books she never finished and
The toys that sucked the family budget dry.

All those years ago before she left in a frenzy
Of hope and luck and enthusiastic goodbyes and "see you soons."

She never thanked them for those nights they waited
Imagining her in twisted knots of wreckage
Unable to return home in time for curfew
But they did not expect it, were so relieved to see her
They forgot those childhood spats, her sibling envy
Secure in the knowledge that the long graduation day
Of endings and beginnings
Had arrived without disaster.

Disconsolate after they have slipped away,
She contemplates her "in-between" existence.
Nothing is quite right here now without them
Her career is just what she was planning
For all those years, but not what she expected
When her parents taught her
All their recipes for success.

But she could never thank them
For that one piece of repetitious advice
She had tuned out as a teenager
And therefore never learned—
To always though the mess—
That is our lives—
Persist.

Morning Rituals

The warm dog sleeps curled by my side,
Dreaming of bacon before the sun comes up.
The smell of coffee stirs my sluggish heart, so
I rise to the radio's tune.
Members of Congress are boasting
About the glorious works
They have recently completed
For the devastated Filipino people,
Suffering in ways I cannot fathom.
As I peel back the covers, I see
An image of defoliated palm trees and ragged clothing,
Then blink it away,
Catch a whiff of excrement and impending disease.
In my half sleep, I creep along downstairs
To rejoin the family dog still snoring softly
On the couch, television blaring.

Nothing but promos for discounted shopping,
Singing of sales and expositions, hot tubs,
Santa Claus, insurance and stealthy
Luxury cars to hold all of our excess, trying to fill up
The void.

I listen to the forecast for our times:/high of 50 degrees/
scattered clouds, no hint of disasters/
the suffering across the globe surely forgotten now/by the
members of Congress-they are so busy/I dress for work/pour
myself another coffee/wonder if I can erase/ what I thought
I saw and smelled/ when I awoke from dreaming with the
lucky dog.

Frenchie Love

Corleen is the baby dog,
Who sniffs everything with an eye
Toward
        Taking its measure
                      As a toy.
Then chews the lucky object
She selects
        With an unrelenting vigor
Born of puppyhood games and
           Dining room chair legs.

My sweet French Bulldog
           Licks my face
In a manner never studied or coy.
There is much we can learn
From her loving and open ways:
How to best appreciate each
And every person and day,
To treasure each other in every kiss,
To nurture the inner puppy in us
We otherwise might have missed.

Teaching the Dog to Pee on the Deck

Getting the dog to pee in the yard
Is very difficult with snow pelting
Her tiny form from every angle.
Who knows what she thinks as she views the world
Covered by a strange white frosting.
Poised in the doorway, she softly touches her well worn pads
To its icy white carpet. Maybe it will refresh her
Afford her that delightful energy, we once observed
When she was young. But no, she returns almost
Immediately, it is too cold for her and she
Mistakenly thinks we are eating something she might like.
Looks up at me with face so forlorn as if
The longing for whatever we might enjoy without her
Is eating her up from the inside.

Impatient now, I motion her outside to try again
On frozen ground, she looks at me stoically through the glass
And waits there patiently without relieving herself.
Sitting in the only spot under the eaves of the house
That is not snow covered. I let her in again, and wait
Some more, until it is almost too late, as night is falling
And I want to go to bed, without worrying about
Her becoming the prey of the fox that roams our yards.
I tell her there is most certainly a COOKIE in it for her
And once again open the door to the night wind.
Despite its gusts, she runs outside, but halts before
Descending the three steps into our yard.
Instead she looks around furtively for a bit,
Then squats on the perfect snow covered deck and lets loose.

As dainty as can be under the circumstances, she dances
Back into the warm house, sits before me and awaits her treat.
The unfortunate lesson in expediency has been a success—
I have finally, on the third try, taught the dog to pee on the deck.

Winter Walk

Wind beating my back,
I plow forth,
My feelings tossed
Far and wide
Across the blue sky.
I hear the drone
Of conversation-
All the world has
Something to say.
I speak in muffled undertones
To myself.

Wind follows me,
A silent eavesdropper
To my mutterings.

All my ideas
Are lost to
All
But the ever listening wind.

I hear its voice
Call back to me,
Screeching obscenities.

In the white light
Brightness of the icy day
I flee,
Running from the force
Pursuing me.

Closer, faster
It presses just
Behind me,
Warning me of its strength.

I fear its muscle
For it is older than I
And tougher than I
And much crueler than I.

I still fear
The faceless wind.
Even protected
By these brick walls
The windows let it in.

Anthem

Spring is here!
I feel the air
Around me
Brighten the sky.
The kitten's eye blueness
Of the atmosphere
Lifts my spirits
For Spring is here.

Spring has risen
As if from the grave
Crocuses and early snowdrops
Form a resurrection
Of innocence and bravery.
I face this morning
With a new hope
Spring has risen—Again.

I sing and join my Robin
Bird friends
I feel their ecstasy
I wish I could nest
In the trees with them
And have no cares,
And hate no one.

I fear the coming of
Winter again,
The coldness, the frozen ground
Under our feet,
The empty and barren streets
People wrapped up like packages
Losing expression, fusing together
Altogether uniform, yet incomplete.

Spring has arrived at last!
My fears are unfounded!
We throw off our wrappings
For the warmth of the sun!
Surely this weather, will bring out
The beauty—in everything, and everyone.

Migration

How miraculous
         This exodus
                Of birds
Off the far lane of the Bay Bridge—
Flying North for Springtime and South for Sanctuary
    Why can't we do the same?

Their wings are grey, blue, lavender vehicles
Of sliding pendency,
        My arms open wide and my
          Expectations are equally high

As they pass through my car's rear view mirror that alters
                    Normalcy—
They emerge on the other side of the span, behind us- in rose,
Orange and green splendor
        And so does my Spring
        Sweet harbingers of Spring.

In Love

Before you came, I had no song
No notes to carry the music within me
Now you are here I sing along
My melody flows pure and clear
Filling the air around us.
We speak of life, of justice and truth,
Our thoughts touch in the darkness.
The unsung ballad I feel in my heart
Initially falters then shakily rises
It grows in one breath to a shimmering
Pitch—
We start with a song, and end in a kiss.

Opera of the Soul

Paper thin the walls
Conscience stricken
The demeanor
She is played like
An instrument
Long unused, brittle, and
Out of tune.

Notes ring harsh
And jar the Conductor.
He waits with patience and fortitude
For the song to commence.

Long forgotten elements of music
Coalesce in an aria so vibrant
It dazzles her mind with
Heat and light, but
The Conductor grows
Impatient
Waiting on the perfect pitch.

My Muse

Nowhere is peace more pronounced
Than in poetry.

While the muse lives, symmetrical words
                Speak volumes
To me.

 I sweep my pen
                    Across blue sky
Reap beauty
        in the
                Constellations.

Ask only if the page is wide-
                Enough to hold
        Imagination.

In the Garden

Only in the garden are we
Free to fall behind.
Inhaling fragrant blossoms
Stirs tranquility divine
There the soul at last is home.

Tasting coral buds and magenta
Petals on the tongue
We laugh our cares away.

Softly feeling their
Pleasure and pain,
We part the velvet planes
Of our roses, we envy
The bees and watch the
Birds fly.

While we remain at bottom
Observers of glory,
Here we dare be
Worshippers of color and light
And life
A garden in May is kind.

Rosebud

June is the wooing month.
I sit atop a lovely seat in nature's
Wild garden on a hill not traveled
Routinely by civilized creatures-
Ah! But...
I close my lids and try to breathe it all in
Everything that has come out into the sun.
The birdsong, the crickets' rasp, the breeze that has been
Crooning to me all along, a rosebud lover's song of rebirth.
Can it be true? Do we have more time to woo
The earth and not just for what we want it to do?
Yes, June's power is on the wing,
Ascending above me in clouds and sky
As I sit, my breathless pleasure astounds my heart

It makes me forget everything, yet still remember—the why.

Beginning

Today is the day that the Lord has made,
So lovely, so resplendent in verdant greens
Warm reds, cool clear blues, and
The soft brown of the sandy soil.
We trespass with our feet
Every time we take a step
Without giving thanks for the glory
Or counting the many blessings
Earth and G-d have left for us.
Ever sweet sleeping animals snore beside me
Lying at my feet and
Paying homage to the very existence
Of unquestioning, unconditional love,
Reminding me how blessed it is to be alive,
Able to live and love all that is before me.
In return, still able to add to the beauty
And motion of life, and be consumed by
Its living flame, drinking in the elixir
Of nature's potent and restoring potion.

Batter Up!

At the ballpark, I strive to forget
All my obsessions, but my regret
Tastes bitter in my mouth at
Every hapless batter out.

Life resembles baseball
Often difficult, unfair
It keeps us swinging
Over and over at
High wide pitches in the air.

In our diligence, we
Train our eyes to watch the ball
Yet on it flies, up and away
From our grasp, after all.

Or down it slides into the
Dirt at our feet.
Sometimes we slink away
Dejected, and take a seat.

Our arms grow sore and tired
With each missed play-
And we grow to settle for a walk
At the close of each long day.

That seemingly endless wait
For the hittable ball
To cross the plate
Imitates frustrated ambition
Swinging wildly, too wide,
And almost too late.

Photography

She shoots from the hip with her camera.
Her photos capture faces of children
Who will never again see
An unmutilated day of peace in their playground.

Her viewfinder saw the day that Spring came,
When the bird song unfurled the petals of flowers and
Green things rose unbidden from the earth's hiding places.
She shot the dandelion instead of the daisy, since it was so
    familiar.
Ordinary yellow on green carpet.

She kept on shooting her film, long after she was asked to stop
When she saw that man being beaten in the street for who
    he was
And for who he might later become as truthful witness.
The internet features her photography, alive in digital color
While she is gone with her camera to another place.

Last I heard of, before the shell that ended it,
She aimed her camera at the birthday party held for a child
In the distant place where rockets are ubiquitous
And mutilations are so common
But daisies and dandelions are never seen at all.

Pandemic Praise Song

Praise the azaleas blooming through the front door glass;
Bless the early morning newscasters, finding new ways to comfort us;
Praise the researchers who are tirelessly looking for treatments;
Bless the participants in every new medical trial;
Praise the teachers who find new ways to continue their avocation;
Praise the parades of their color clad graduates;
Bless the online Proms and Concerts without cease;
Praise the mothers and fathers who are teaching their children lessons of kindness and civic duty, rather than cruelty and selfishness;
Bless the first responders and the heroic medical workers for their unceasing bravery;
Praise all the essential workers who risk everything, everyday, for everyone;
Bless the meditators who calm us;
Praise the mediators who unite us;
Bless the unselfish mask wearers who seek to protect others despite discomfort;
Bless the civil servants who telework to keep our country from collapsing around us;
Praise the mechanics who fix our cars so we can travel when needed;
Bless those in nursing homes who need our assistance;
Praise the vaccinators for helping us inoculate the public;
Bless those who are alone, for their fortitude and bless them with all forms of recovery;
Praise everyone still telling the truth to power;

And bless the sky, blue and boundless in Springtime, and the
   star filled infinite heavens, seen through doors, windows,
   and everywhere else, easing our
collective pain—through their unceasing connection to the
   universe.

Workaday Plea....

Thursdays are sad days, not quite week's end, they mark the strain
Of work days gone long, too little accomplished, and too much rain
In the forecast. Even the pain of toil gone wrong
Cannot erase the stain of the almost right,
Stunted by dreary lack of light and seemingly endless chores to come.
I say a small prayer to the creator of lighthearted fun:
Oh, help us to complete the week and pull back the heavy drapes that creak
And ever so slowly slide the weekend forward to where we are,
Trembling with anticipation, waiting in the still glum dark,
When finally, the light shines on the work of the human heart.

Ah, the weekend, balm of my soul, food of the ever young.
Clearly, that is when all our most important loving and living will be done.

Something is Coming

The ocean laps the seagrasses upon the
Shell shattered beaches
And carries the smallest fish
To and fro in the foam
Into the Dolphins'
Waiting mouths.
The ocean brings the sea turtles
Back to their seasonal beach-side nests.
It cares for their issue
And for the majestic singing whales
Whose calls are lately drowned out
By sonar signals in the deep.

But—the ocean does not care
If you are a wealthy oligarch
Or an unruly unkempt member
Of the masses (aka the rest of us)
It does not worry about your next
Medical appointment
Or your Landlord
Or your taxes
Or whether you are dressed appropriately
For the time and place- or even your age.

The ocean does not ponder
The fresh indignities
At your job
Or riding in your car
Or at your school or social club.

It does not wonder, as you do,
Whether you have funds available
To pay the rent and electricity bill and
Still prepare dinner for your family tonight.

It also does not care what is going on in
Your daughter in law's house,
Or the hospital you visited last week.

The ocean does not care what cruise vessels
Ply their way across it or whether you are
Unexpectedly and dramatically
Pulled off your ticketed flight
On the way to that cruise,
By overzealous airline police.

It does not even worry too much
About our futile efforts at desalinization
Before we run out of clean freshwater
For our planet's population.
It does not dream about rising dunes
That could protect the coastline from erosion.
These days, it does not seem to notice
how many dolphins and sea turtles
Get tangled in fishing nets
With the tuna and crab legs.

The ocean may not even notice
What is being dumped in it daily.

When the flood finally arrives,
The ocean will be vicious in its neutrality
Reacting with an unparalleled
Climate based vengeance
Born of our uncaring, selfish,
And inexplicably
Backwards leaning ways,
Dispensing justice at last
In the face of our "progress."

Spider Land

Trailing golden plume of silky ash
she rises above catastrophe.
Hovering over uncertain depths
she spins her way past the places
I frequented in my youth,
A tight rope weaver ever
in pursuit.
Evading the last gasp of those
final summer wasp venom pools
She at last is at home
in her harmonious woven den.
Every stitch recalls a battle
lost to aging karma.
When she slips the knot past my waist,
I can no longer plan my escape,
pulling at the threads of destiny
across the miles of cord and memory,
She is bound to bind me.
The end is but the circle of the path
on a cloudless day, we now embrace.

Off the Boardwalk

I.

Beauty on the beach, I love your ease of repose,
Your lassitude mocks my efficient breezy gait
As I walk by, stop here and wait
For your awakening.
Surely the rays
Of the sun at play
On your recumbent pose
Will make all that
Sleeps and dreams
In the light of the day
And the peace of the sea
Wake and smell clear as when
I first felt your absence,
Yet saw your form sleeping here.

II.

That first dinner, we were so happy together.
Children played just outside our earshot
On the beach, yet we did not hear them.
We talked all manner of things and spoke our heart's delight
We did not notice the smoke, the mirrors, the things
Lurking just outside our line of sight.
But later, much later, when the night
Crept in, we remembered what we came here for
And were soothed by the soft quiet
Of the seemingly depthless water
Here at our beach house by the shore.

III.

She is trying to catch a glimpse of the ocean
Walking past the grey bulk of souls in motion.
She looks over her shoulder and spies an opening,
Yet she turns instead to greet me with her sad eyes.
In her watching face I see something that is clearly unlike
The collection of featureless frames she tries
To emulate with all her might.
But maybe she spies a final dolphin on the wave
And longs to fly past the long wall of human pain
To the waiting pool of the silver sand and sky.

French Fry Finality

The very last fry she ate,
on the beach trip she had earned,
approximated her hard life.
She wondered, as the burning spread upward,
how it could still be so soft on the inside.

The fry patiently bore
submersion,
in bubbling peanut oil,
until finally released
and poured into the paper container,
virtually oozing its crisp salty flavor
at the precise moment of its end.

When she thought about how she would go,
she imagined a car/plane/train wreck,
an industrial accident,
a tumor in her breast,
maybe even a broken heart.

Surrendering to the spreading darkness,
she tasted the still warm melt
of the fry's vinegar saltiness.

In that final moment,
before she collapsed on the boardwalk,
she regretted that although her life had been
filled with warm and salty tastes,
she had never properly learned how to cook.

Celestial Ground Search

That night we were snug
in our northern beds
dreaming of the storm
whistling past
our beautiful islands
of erstwhile paradise.

But where were you,
creator of tiny babies
and the beautiful scent of frangipani?
Did you not spy us down on our knees,
O' Protector of tropical trees,
and coral reefs
and colorful fish without number?

Were you also sleeping as the wind
ripped roofs from fearful
families huddling against
one another for comfort
in the dark?

How did you not hear the wind
screaming its relentless song—
of murder and distress?
Were you there beside the woman
captured by video
who cried out
as buildings built by man
shook around her
and collapsed—
burying hundreds
of innocent souls?

Where were you
when the chemical plants
in that Texas town were erupting
in "controlled" explosions
and the levees were loosened
to flood
whole soccer family
neighborhoods
with dark water?

We saw the lifeboats
of neighbors
and the kindnesses
of strangers
doing your job
rescuing thousands
of our brothers
and sisters and animals,
from the tainted flood waters,
but did not see you anywhere!

Maybe you are directing
the helicopters dropping food
to feed the islands
to the tune of
heavenly harmonies above.
But you are so hard to see
in the pitch darkness
where we reside below
where all we can currently hear
is the sound of trees
snapping
and wires whipping,
and transformers
like gunshots
exploding everywhere.

Envy

Driving by in the sunshine,
the other day
in my tired grey Toyota,
I passed a bay house.

It rose up in serene splendor
from the sea grasses.
Their fluffy heads strained
just high enough
to obscure the entry point,
but its windows winked at me.

For a second, I dreamed
I was an invited guest,
though there was no way inside.
Failing to enter, I mused
that its inhabitants,
unaware of their entrapment,
but enjoying the view,
forgot to build
the doorstep.

Holes

In the donut shop, I sit
Trying to recall the reasons I love anyone at all.
The soft warm taste of avoidance in my gut, I think
I am ready to leave everything behind, but then
I hear your voice again telling me last night
How we have always loved one another and that
We always would.

I look at all the photos on my phone
Documenting some of the events of our lives.
Parties, dinners, walks in the park.
Not too many selfies, as we already
Thought we knew who we were.

Now, in the doctor's office I again sit,
Trying to recall why I ever thought a physician could
Assist in curing my disappointment with all things.
This over and over again feeling not quite as we should.
Why do they make us sit up high on a table, like we are young,
When the sagging skin on our faces shows us we grow older
   by the minute?
Did you ever think that your suffering would be someone
   else's dull job?

So that is why I so often find myself in the donut shop,
Avoiding difficult thoughts by biting into
That comforting taste of sweetness.
Yet, it leaves a gritty feeling on the tongue.
Why do we always bite the donut? I suddenly posit—
Oh, nutty philosopher that I am.

Once we eat it, we remain sad as ever.
Would it not be better, to chastely notice its perfume in the air,
Slake our satisfaction from that deep breath of chocolate glaze,
And harvest our hope from the feel of the powdered sugar on
Our fingers?

Never again tasting the holes.

Day and Night

Morning grumbles
Stretching its brightly hued arms
Above its head,
Yawning with mouth wide and teeth white
In the growing sunshine.
Head cleared, it sings out boldly
Daring all living things to follow
This example.

The night is feared for it is darkly sighing
Does not sing but holds its broken tune within.
It wakes the guilty and the sleeping child
And stirs the unlit passages in the poet's mind.

Foreboding

Here is a Sunday
One day filled with
Left to the last minute
Chores of dread.

Senselessly, we storm about
In circles to soundly
Tuck in the sheets and
Make our bed for the
Coming sleepwalked week.

And then on Monday—
We lie in it.
The potential of it all
Rests heavily on our eyelids.

The shame of last Friday's
Misdeeds still stings
Fresh in our minds.

Imagined tears burn our
Pupils and spill into
Monday morning's coffee
As we prepare to face the mess ahead.

Cyclone

Dreaming of things that crawl beneath us
Hearing the stir of the under world
My beloved pet slips from my grasp
Into the placid lake of glass
I cannot swim.

My home grows extra rooms I never knew before
Ripe for aimless darkened wanderings
Through paths I would not travel while awake
My long gone grandmother tries to tell me something
I strain to hear her moan.

A large Oz shaped balloon, traces hills and follows river
Dipping down into its depths so slightly as I
Stagger my breath, to fit its cadence
Of light air and pendent rhyme
The up and down slide
Kneads my tight muscles
Like the cyclone
Its in and out,
Back and forth
Movement
Is divine.

But next I see my death whitened body
Outside an eerie glowing home I recognize
Ripped apart by wolves I yet remember
From my mother's hospital room
They would not let her die.
Yet I wake with a start,
With that overwhelming sense of gloom,
As if my mind remains in a windowless place
Taking that test I always fail,
You know the one.....

It is a very bad night to dream of doom.

Night Terrors

They sang while I was asleep,
Rested paper thin translucent wings
On my eyes until I dreamed of their flight.
I could not wake—each time my lids cracked open.
I felt them press me down.

When I was ten, I saw bubbles fill the air
With the bobbing of tissued things.
I walked though their world without understanding.
Barely visible, yet they marked my path.
My hands passed through them, floating.
Were they fairy or fey, a trick of the eyes?
Midnight or daylight, I could not rest easy.
I wondered why they followed me everywhere.

Later, when I tried, I couldn't summon them
Or guess their purpose.

Now, they show up in photos
Through ovals of light,
Nonexistent in the camera's view.
My daughter posits they are spirits
Floating around us for protection.
I offer my own ideas—a smudge on the lens,
Anything but those night terrors again.

Do they only follow until we forget
The magic that brought us here—or
Do they only depart when we accept
That our world no longer offers
Anything we cannot see through?

Pack Rat

Have you ever thought about -the things that linger?
The detritus of daily life, those old styrofoam fast food
 containers
I still find in my daughter's room.
She used them to fill her up.
The paper clips we buy to futilely try
holding things together,
The pens that, lacking ink, or those tiny necessary springs,
end up at the bottoms of drawers, mixed with
old handwritten address books.
My closets are filled with dry cleaner bags.
Piles of single socks adorn my dresser.
I find unexpired gift cards in unexpected places.

My husband found my grandmother's rug
the other day
in a box
mailed to me weeks after her death
by my now dead uncle.
I could not bear to open it then.
It lingered in our attic until,
by the miracle of winter clearing out,
we found it once again.

I was surprised when it reappeared
in a new stage of our lives
after so many other ties have passed.
Their things linger long after their physical presence departs.

I saw my fractious daughter the other night.
As she sat across from me
eating hearty on my dime
in that chain restaurant she likes.

Telling me she will only make herself happy
by traveling far from her troubles.
I made sure I told her "Wherever you go, there you are."
Most things follow us, eventually.

It is hard to know what we can safely keep.
Fearful of letting go,
We hold onto things that slip away.
Others linger though we try to cast them off.

But that lovely rug my grandmother hooked by hand
is of great comfort to me now as I walk barefoot upon it.
Call me "pack rat" but I cannot seem
to discard the paper wrapping with my uncle's handwriting.
When I close my eyes, I can see him again,
addressing it to me with tears in his kind blue eyes.
Doesn't everything have some final use after all?

To Walt Whitman

Liquid movement flows through your words
As blood pulses in our veins
You connect the altogether so completely
There is no room for mistake or accident
Your all is perfect and predestined.

Together we share your every perception
As if it were our own
Spatial relationships bow
To the continuum of poetic verse.
Through the leaves, the blades of grass or otherwise
Deep feelings within us are personified.

Magic, as though through faerie touch—
We are all kin.
What spell to cast a beam of truth
Over each of us?
In desperate dreams, we seek the stars
Only to touch the gravel beneath our feet.
Then despairing, we turn to G-d
For an answer.

Sadly, it has taken us centuries to begin
To realize
That love is truth, not fear.

Resolution

Never defeated, I will transcend
Every obstacle in my path.
I will defend
My unquenchable drive
To rise above the
Petty issues of the fray.

I will laugh at negative thoughts
I place in my way.
I will leave failure behind
For another distant day.

I may stumble across the
Threshold of success, unsure
I have reached my goal

But I will triumph
In spite of everything,
And smile again, after all.

www.ingramcontent.com/pod-product-compliance
Lightning Source LLC
Chambersburg PA
CBHW051701040426
42446CB00009B/1244